Dot.

with much love
for Christmas 1990.

Nicola

EDEN

EDEN

GRAPHICS and POETRY
by
CHARLES TOMLINSON

Redcliffe Poetry

Bristol

First published by
Redcliffe Press Ltd.,
49 Park St.,
Bristol BS1 5NT

ISBN 0 948265 00 0

Typeset by Folio Phototypesetting, Bristol
Printed and bound by South Western Printers Ltd., Caerphilly

To Brenda

ACKNOWLEDGEMENTS

I am grateful to Oxford University Press for granting permission to print the selection of poems and to Will Sulkin and Corinna Mitchell in particular for their kind help and efficient co-operation. I thank Jonathan Barker and Andrew Dempsey whose original selection for an Arts Council exhibition of graphics and poems was the starting point for this book. Michael Abbott from Redcliffe Press has proved consistently helpful in shaping the volume. Thanks are also due to Richard Ings from South-West Arts and to Martin Haswell for extra photography.

The essay 'The Poet as Painter' is based upon a lecture originally given to the Royal Society of Literature (Essays by Divers Hands: Volume XL, 1979).

WITH THE ASSISTANCE OF

SOUTH WEST ARTS

CONTENTS

OPENINGS

THE POET AS PAINTER

'We live in the centre of a physical poetry,' says Wallace Stevens. This is surely the basic fact which would make a poet want to paint or, if he couldn't do that, to comprehend the painter's way of regarding the physical poetry they both share. It is because of this same basic fact of '[living] in the centre of a physical poetry' that Samuel Palmer's follower, Edward Calvert, could write of 'a good poem whether written or painted'. 'To a large extent,' says Stevens, 'the problems of poets are the problems of painters, and poets must often turn to the literature of painting for a discussion of their own problems.' One could add to this remark of Stevens that they not only turn to the literature of painting, but help create that literature.

Stevens' *Opus Posthumous* has for its epigraph a passage by Graham Bell on the integrity of Cézanne, a painter Stevens has commented on memorably more than once. Besides Stevens, Rainer Maria Rilke, D. H. Lawrence, William Carlos Williams are all poets who have written penetratingly about Cézanne. All found in him a reflection of their own problems as writers as they fought preconception and subjectivity in their art. 'It is the crisis in these paintings that I recognised,' says Rilke, 'because I had reached it in my own work.' And D. H. Lawrence: 'Cézanne felt it in paint, when he felt for the apple. Suddenly he felt the tyranny of mind, the enclosed ego in its sky-blue heaven self-painted.' And Williams: 'Cézanne – The only realism in art is of the imagination. It is only thus that the work escapes plagiarism after nature and becomes a creation.' So Cézanne looms gigantically over literature as well as over painting, as the forerunner of a new sensibility and a new inventiveness. Indeed, Cézanne – to traverse the common ground between poet and painter in the other direction – composed many poems of his own. As a young man, he wrote:

> A tree, shaken by raging winds,
> Waves in the air, like a gigantic corpse,
> Its naked branches which the mistral sways.

As an old man, he made good this vision in an astonishing water colour that acquired the title 'Bare Trees in the Fury of the Wind'. Whatever the final product, the point of departure was the same: 'We live in the centre of a physical poetry'.

To Cézanne and his meaning for poetry I shall return. But, first, let me add a subtitle to my essay which will permit me to explore the centre of that physical poetry in which Stevens says we live. My subtitle is 'The Four Elements' and the place of my exploration, the Potteries where I was born. The element that touched most persistently on the imagination there of the child as growing artist, was water. For that region of smoke and blackened houses, of slag-heaps, cinder-paths, pitheads, steelworks, had for its arterial system a network of canals. The canals brought back the baptismal element to a landscape by day purgatorial and by night infernal. The canals were not the only bringers of water into that place whose atmosphere, according to Arnold Bennett, was as black as its mud. One must not forget the great pools that formed in the pits where marl was dug for tile-making: as the pits were gradually abandoned, nature re-invaded, greenness appeared beside the water and fish in it. Fish! It was their existence, not just in the marl pools, but in the canals, that helped bring back contemplation into lives lived-out in the clatter of mines and factories. The fishing-club, the Sunday matches, long hours watching the rufflings and changes of water, something both sane and mysterious came from all this. Why mysterious? Because the fisherman, if he is to be more than a random dabbler, must acquire an intuitive knowledge of the ways of fish and water, and within his stillness, at the centre of his capacity to wait and to contemplate, there is a sense that is ready to strike at the exact moment, that even knows, perhaps, how to lure into its own mental orbit creatures that he cannot even see under that surface on which his whole attention is concentrated. Piscator is an artist, as Walton knew. His discipline, looking out from himself but with his inner faculties deeply roused, might make a poet or painter of him if he had the latent powers within.

So much for water. What of earth and fire in this same Midland childhood? 'The district' – the Potteries, that is – says Bennett 'comprehends the mysterious habits of fire and pure, sterile earth.' He means, of course, the action of fire on the potting clay. My own most remembered and most dwelt on experience of the physical poetry of fire concerns the making of steel rather than the making of pots. And it was an experience, principally, of fire by night. When the furnaces were tapped by night, or when molten metal was poured in the great open sheds of the steel works, immense dazzling shafts of fire flared outwards to be reflected in the waters of the nearby canal. Thus the remembered experience was also of fire associated with water, of fire not as the opposite of water, but mingling with it, kindling reflections in that element and also in the onlooker. To see was also to see *within*.

You gained this experience by following the canal beyond the factory established by Josiah Wedgwood in the eighteenth century, in the place named by him Etruria. You went on until the canal cut through the centre of the Shelton Bar-Iron and Steel Works. And you went by night, so as not to be seen , because children were not particularly welcome there. Etruria – Etruria Vale to give it its full name – had long since lost the nymphs one might associate with the name. But the red jets and glarings from molten steel, and from the furnaces seen in the canal, confronted one with a sense of the primal and the elemental such as nymphs themselves were once thought to symbolise in relation to landscape. And, after all, a dryad would only be a veil between yourself and a tree once your eyes had been opened by this other intenser nakedness. For, with the soot drifting down through the darkness on to your hair, you had experienced fire as the interior of water.

Earth, like air, fared badly in the district. 'Its atmosphere as black as its mud': Bennett's verdict. Earth, like air, took on the tinge of blackness. Earth was close to the sterile earth not only of pots but of slag-heaps and cinderpaths. For all that, gardeners coaxed miracles out of the sooty allotments that crowned the slopes where Etruria Woods had once flourished. As for air – air was something of a joke. There were local post-cards showing bottle-ovens and factory chimneys all smoking at once with dark hints of houses and perhaps a drab church-tower. These cards carried stoical titles like, 'Fresh Air from the Potteries'. At school, when the potteries 'stoked-up', it was sometimes difficult to see over to the far side of the playground. A familiar image returns from that time, of black smoke mounting from a factory chimney and, caught by the wind, fraying out across and into the air. Air was an element that yet had to be created there. It was, in part, the search for air, as well as water, that drew the fishing clubs out to the surrounding countryside, still along those canals, that seemed to lead back to Eden.

So of the four elements it was water that held the imagination of the child as growing artist – water fire-tinged, water promising a cleansing, an imaginative baptism, rocking, eddying, full of metamorphoses.

I left the district in my early twenties and subsequently lived among many landscapes both urban and rural – London, Italy, New Mexico, the northern

United States, the Cotswolds. I think it was Liguria and Tuscany and then Gloucestershire taught me the way men could be at home in a landscape. And how necessary this different view of things was, in order to place those earlier experiences of streets that threatened to enclose you, to shut you off from a wider and more luminous world, from intuitions of what Ezra Pound calls 'the radiant world where one thought cuts through another with clear edge, a world of moving energies, magnetisms that take form . . .' I wanted to recover that 'radiant world' in poems, and by doing so I seemed to have lost touch with the Midlands. But the Midlands were always present as one term in a dialectic, as a demand for completeness subconsciously impelling the forms of one's art, even demanding *two* arts where the paradisal aspect of the visual could perhaps be rescued and celebrated.

Coming back to the Potteries almost thirty years later, I saw how much the world of my poems depended on the place, despite and because of the fact that they were an attempt to find a world of clarities, a world of unhazed senses, an intuition of Edenic freshnesses and clear perceptions. I tried to concentrate the history of all that into one short poem, *The Marl Pits* (see p.25).

Can my 'psychoanalysis of water', to appropriate a term of Gaston Bachelard's, point to any single prompting insight, any happy combination of perception and intuition that unifies the attitudes of poet and painter? Pondering this question, I remembered an early poem, *Sea Change*, formally quite simple in that it seeks to catch the nature of water – this time, the sea – in a series of images, 'uneasy marble', 'green silk', 'blue mud', then is forced to concede their inadequacy: they are like

> white wine
> Floating in a saucer of ground glass
> On a pedestal of cut glass:
>
> A static instance, therefore untrue.

Much later – the better part of twenty years later – in a formally much more complex poem, *Swimming Chenango Lake*, I watch a swimmer watching water. This is an extract from the opening:

> Winter will bar the swimmer soon.
>   He reads the water's autumnal hesitations
> A wealth of ways: it is jarred,
>   It is astir already despite its steadiness,
> Where the first leaves at the first

> Tremor of the morning air have dropped
> Anticipating him, launching their imprints
>   Outwards in eccentric, overlapping circles.
> There is a geometry of water, for this
>   Squares off the clouds' redundances
> And sets them floating in a nether atmosphere
>   All angles and elongations: every tree
> Appears a cypress as it stretches there
>   And every bush that shows the season,
> A shaft of fire. It is a geometry and not
>   A fantasia of distorting forms, but each
> Liquid variation answerable to the theme
>   It makes away from, plays before:
> It is a consistency, the grain of the pulsating flow . . .

I pondered this passage, along with that earlier poem *Sea Change*, to find out the constant that governed my attitude as poet and painter. Poems based like this – as are the many landscape poems I have written – on exposure to and observation of the fleeting moments of visual sensation; poems that endeavour to catch this fleeting freshness and unite it to a stable form where others may share in it; poems such as these look away from the merely personal. And so does painting where the presence of the external world is strongly felt, where the painter is concerned – I quote Rilke on Cézanne – with 'the incarnation of the world *as a thing carrying conviction*, the portrayal of a reality become imperishable through his experiencing of the object'. To make the reality of water imperishable! The painter must acquire great formal power to achieve that: because he who looks into water, and into the changing world of perception which water represents, looks into the heart of time.

Cézanne himself was very conscious of this problem for the painter – how to reconcile sensation and form without bullying your picture into a wilful unity, a triumph of personality at the expense of a truth to relationship: 'There mustn't be a single link too loose,' Joachim Gasquet reports him as saying, 'not a crevice through which may escape the emotion, the light, the truth . . . All that we see disperses, vanishes; is it not so? Nature is always the same, but nothing remains of it, nothing of what comes to our sight. Our art ought to give the shimmer of duration with the elements, the appearance of all its changes. It ought to make us taste it eternally . . . My canvas joins hands . . . But if I feel the least distraction, the least weakness, above all if I intepret too much one day . . . if I intervene, why then everything is gone.'

Long before I read that conversation with Gasquet, I wrote a poem called *Cézanne at Aix* (see p. 38), a kind of manifesto poem where I wanted my poetry to take its ethic of perception from Cézanne, an ethic distrustful of the drama of personality of which Romantic art had made so much, an ethic where, by trusting to sensation, we enter being, and experience its primal fulness on terms other than those we dictate.

What impressed me about Cézanne, and what on my own humbler level I wanted for poetry, was the entire absence of self-regard. 'Cézanne's apples,' says D. H. Lawrence, 'are a real attempt to let the apple exist in its own separate entity, without transfusing it with personal emotion.' Cézanne must surely have felt the narrowing lure of what Lawrence calls 'personal emotion' here. Cézanne *in himself* was threatened by misunderstanding, neglect, ill-health and prone to deep melancholy. Had he chosen to ignore nature or merely to dramatise that self and impose it on nature, his pictures would have wanted the liberating Mediterranean radiance that we find there. Even his self-portraits lack introspection. Rilke, once more, supplies the classic comment. He writes to his wife: ' . . . how great and incorruptible this objectivity of his gaze was, is confirmed in an almost touching manner by the circumstance that, without analysing or in the remotest degree regarding his expression from a superior standpoint, he made a replica of himself with so much humble objectiveness, with the credulity of extrinsic interest and attention of a dog which sees itself in the mirror and thinks: there is another dog.'

In speaking of Cézanne's incorruptible objectivity, it is clear that Rilke was not thinking of the purely imaginary and outmoded objectivity of nineteenth century positivistic science – the objectivity which supposed a complete division between the observer and the observed. The objectivity with which Rilke credits Cézanne implied an outward gaze that would draw the sensuous world closer to the inner man and that would narrow the gap between abstraction and sensation, between intellect and things. As Merleau-Ponty reflects in his great essay, 'Eye and Mind' – an essay that begins by quoting Gasquet's book on Cézanne –: 'Quality, light, colour, depth which are there before us, are there only because they awaken an echo in our body and because the body welcomes them . . . Things have an internal equivalent in me; they arouse in me a carnal formula of their presence.' So much for Merleau-Ponty. I wanted to earn the right to use the artistic ethic of Cézanne as a basis for poetry, and I believe it made possible to me a range from natural landscape to civic landscape. It seemed to me a sort of religion, a bringing of things to stand in the light of origin, a way, even, of measuring the tragic fall from plenitude in our own urban universe. But let me make a confession. As a painter, I could find no direct way of using this inheritance. I confronted the four elements, but the only way I could resolve them in paint was to will their cohesion, to intervene, to put personal pressure on my forms in the shape of an anxious black outline. Time and again, I would approach the expression of some realisation, only to disfigure it with black. I could find no way of letting the given suggest to me forms that could elude the preconceptions of the too conscious mind and the too conscious hand, blackening nature as surely as the factory chimneys of my boyhood had blackened it. Black became an obsession. Although I continued to draw, little by little I lapsed from painting, partly under pressure from this insoluble dilemma, partly because the time that might have gone to finding an answer went into earning a living. For fifteen years, almost nothing except the poems; then, in 1970, after a renewed, intensive spell of drawing, a solution appeared almost casually.

I think, once more, of Wallace Stevens, and that entry in his *Adagia* which reads: 'The aspects of earth of interest to a poet are the casual ones, as light or colour, images'. By 'casual', I take it that he refers to the fortuitous nature of art – the way one may find its deepest meanings on a dull street corner, in an old pair of shoes, in the chance conjunction of the totally unforeseen and the apparently unrelated. Suddenly things knit up – the canvas joins hands, in Cézanne's words. You cease to impose and you discover, to rephrase another aphorism of Stevens. And you discover apparently by chance. But what is chance? And if one accepts it, does it not cease to be chance?

The element of chance that helped resolve my problems as a painter was the surrealist device known as decalcomania. Briefly, the recipe for this is the one drawn up by Oscar Dominguez in 1936: 'By means of a thick brush, spread out black gouache more or less diluted in places, upon a sheet of glossy white paper, and cover at once with a second sheet, upon which exert an even pressure. Lift off the second sheet without haste.' Well, the result of this process, as the pigment separates out into random patterns, can be a lot of wasted paper, occasionally a very beautiful entire image, sometimes interesting fragments that prompt and defy the imagination to compose them into a picture. You can alter what is given with a brush, or you can both alter and recombine your images by going to work with scissors and paste and making a collage. The weakness of this technique is that it can lead to a flaccid fantasy of imaginary animals, or of lions turning into bicycles. Its strength lies in its challenge to mental sets, in the very impersonality of the material offered you and that you must respond to. A very unCézannian undertaking, and yet what I have called the ethic of Cézanne – submission to the given, the desire to break with preconceived images of the given, the desire to seize on and stabilize momentary appearances – this ethic, once applied, can lead your decalcomania away from the arbitrariness of fantasy towards the threshold of new perceptions.

I had followed Dominguez very literally: 'Spread out black gouache,' he says. Max Ernst, using this technique for the basis of some of his best pictures, clearly employs several colours. Almost blindly, I reached for my old enemy, black, I continued to use it and to use that colour only. The first move was to paint the black on to a wet surface and the first thing you saw was the strokes of pigment fraying out into the water just as the smoke of your childhood had frayed out into the air. There seemed an odd rhyme here between the one experience and the other. And as I covered sheet on sheet, altered, blotted, painted with brush, finger-tips, pieces of string, and then cut up and recombined, I saw black become dazzling: I saw the shimmer of water, light and air take over from the merely fortuitous: I saw that I was working now as poet *and* painter once more.

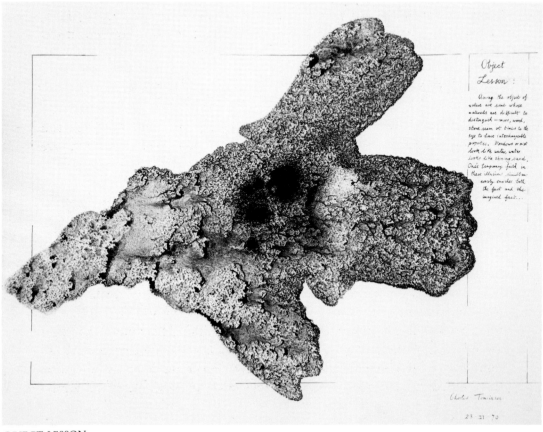

OBJECT LESSON

The 'merely' fortuitous! *There* is a theme for them both: the fact that 'chance' rhymes with 'dance' is a nutrifying thought for either poet or painter. As is that other fortuity, that in the south of England, they are pronounced 'darnce' and 'charnce', a source of wonder to the Midlander, as no doubt *his* pronounciation is to the southerner. There seems no intrinsic reason why these two words should have much to do with each other. And there seems no intrinsic reason, either, why the strokes of a brush covered in pigment, the dabbing of a paint-covered finger, the dashes, slashes or dots a painter makes, should have much to do with a face, a landscape, a stone or a skull. Turner grew an immensely long eagle's talon of a thumb-nail in order to scratch out lights in his water-colours. It seems oddly fortuitous that these jabbings into the surface of water-colour paper should come to represent luminosity.

'Chance' undoubtedly rhymes with 'dance' and meditation on this fact feeds the mind: chance occurrences, chance meetings invade what we do every day and yet they are drawn into a sort of pattern, as they criss-cross with our feeling of what we are, as they remind us of other happenings, or strengthen our sense of future possibility. Poetry is rather like this, also. Something seemingly fortuitous sets it off – a title, say, out of the blue, asking for a poem to go with it, a title like 'The Chances of Rhyme' and you find yourself writing on the back of an envelope:

> The chances of rhyme are like the chances of meeting –
> In the finding fortuitous, but once found binding . . .

Already, you have started to knit up those chances, with 'finding' and 'binding' reinforcing the pattern and before long the chances of rhyme are becoming the continuities of thought, and you continue writing:

> To take chances, as to make rhymes
> Is human, but between chance and impenitence
> (A half rhyme) come dance, vigilance
> And circumstance . . .

Yes, that makes sense. It seems to be getting somewhere: a pattern in the words, a pattern in the thought, a pattern in the way the line settles mostly for four main stresses, sometimes stretches to five, mostly dances back to four. To handle measure thus seems a human thing to do: your recurrences are never so pat as to seem simply mechanical, your outgrowths never so rambling or brambled as to spread to mere vegetation. A human measure, surrounded by surprises, impenetrables and unknowables, but always reasserting itself, this could be a salutary aim – one in which rhythm and tone are both allies –, faced as we always are by the temptation to exaggerate and to overvalue the claims of self (see p. 42).

Painting wakes up the hand, draws-in your sense of muscular co-ordination, your sense of the body, if you like. Poetry also, as it pivots on its stresses, as it rides forward over the line-endings, or comes to rest at pauses *in* the line, poetry also brings the whole man into play and his bodily sense of himself. But there is no near, actual equivalent in painting for tone and rhythm adjusted by line lengths and by pauses within and at the ends of lines. There is no near equivalent because the medium is so very different. You may write with a pencil, but once you come to draw with it, what a diverse end those marks serve. But the fortuitous element is still there – the element of meeting something you didn't expect, something that isn't yourself. And once you attend to it, whatever you are starts to see an interesting challenge to its own relaxed complacency. Quite by accident you find, on a beach, the skull of a sea bird, for instance. You could put it in a glass cabinet or forget it in a safe place, but instead you draw it. You begin to know far more about the structure of that particular skull, as eye and pencil try to keep up with each other.

There is a lot, though, you can't know about – the mysterious darkness of its interior, the intriguing and impenetrable holes and slots where something or other has now rotted away and left a clean emptiness. The cleanliness, the natural geometry of the skull suggest the idea of surrounding it in a geometry of your own – carefully ruled lines that set off the skull, that extend it, that bed it in a universe of contrasting lines of force. Just as rhyme dancing with thought led you through to a world of human values, so skull and line build up and outwards into a containing universe.

Now, there is something very resistant about this skull. You feel you could etch a very tiny poem on it called, perhaps, 'To be Engraved on the Skull of a Cormorant'. To do so you would have to be both tough and careful with it –

> . . . as searching as the sea
> that picked and pared
> this head yet spared
> its frail acuity.

And so you go on to write a poem (see p. 30). But that interior darkness goes on bothering you. How could I relate it, you think, to the little universe my lines netted together around it?

This particular problem was solved by forgetting about it. Or by seeming to forget and doing something else. Three years after making a drawing, 'Long-beaked Skull', I did a decalcomania-collage called 'The Sleep of Animals': here two skulls are filled by a dream of the landscapes the bird and animal presences have been moving through. The dream articulates the darkness. I try to suggest a whole world in each head. There is the hint that this sleep is, perhaps, death in which both the head and nature are now one.

In writing poetry, you sometimes run aground on silence, and it takes months or sometimes years to learn what it is you wish to say. In the meantime, you are half-consciously turning the problem over, while, at the same time, furthering the knowledge of your medium. Among the techniques I had worked with between 'Long-beaked Skull' and 'The Sleep of Animals' were those I have described – collage and decalcomania. I had suddenly seen something rather like – though not yet *much* like – two skulls merged in the landscape of my decalcomania, my chaos of crushed pigment floating in water. Instead of continuing to paint, once the sheet had dried, I cut out the skulls with scissors, glued new shapes onto them, then fitted

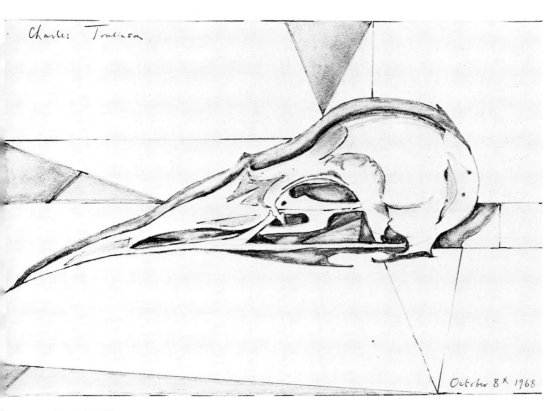

Charles Tomlinson

October 8ᵗʰ 1968

LONG BEAKED SKULL

them into a quite rigorous design held together by ruled lines and called it 'The Sleep of Animals'. I realised I had discovered a response to the dark, unenterable interior of that first bird's skull. My response seemed to have arrived instantaneously, but – again like poetry – the formal pattern had taken up chance elements, had been the result of conscious and sub-conscious processes and of that strange, unifying movement of recognition when, reaching for the scissors, what I'd found became what I'd chosen. 'Chance' rhymed with 'dance' once more.

Why, as an artist, should one return so obsessively to the shape of the skull, whether animal or human? I do not believe that one comes back to it merely as a memento mori – though *that* element is present too. What seems equally important is the skull seen as a piece of architecture. It resembles a house with lit façade and shadowy interior. However much it possesses of bleak finality, it always involves one in the fascination of inside and outside, that primary lure of the human mind seeking to go beyond itself, taking purchase on the welcoming or threatening surfaces of the world, and both anxious and enriched because of the sense of what lies behind or beneath those surfaces. I tried to make this knowledge present to myself in many drawings, particularly of animal skulls. I tried, also, to articulate this knowledge with words, in the form of a poem-in-prose called *Skullshapes*, (see p. 34).

In both graphic and poetic art, I like something lucid surrounded by something mysterious. I see poems and pictures as the place where the civilised, discriminating faculties and the sense of the elemental, of origins, reinforce each other. I go back, time and again, to the idea of a seascape

> with illegible depths
> and lucid passages,
> bestiary of stones,
> book without pages . . .

and a poem seems to be composing itself that could well be a picture, or several pictures (see *On Water* p. 57).

When words seem too abstract, then I find myself painting the sea with the very thing it is composed of – water, and allowing its thinning and separation of the pigment to reveal an image of its own nature. I spoke earlier of bringing things to stand in the light of origin. When you paint with water and are painting the image of water, you return to it, as to all primal things, with a sense of recognition – water! we came from this. 'Human

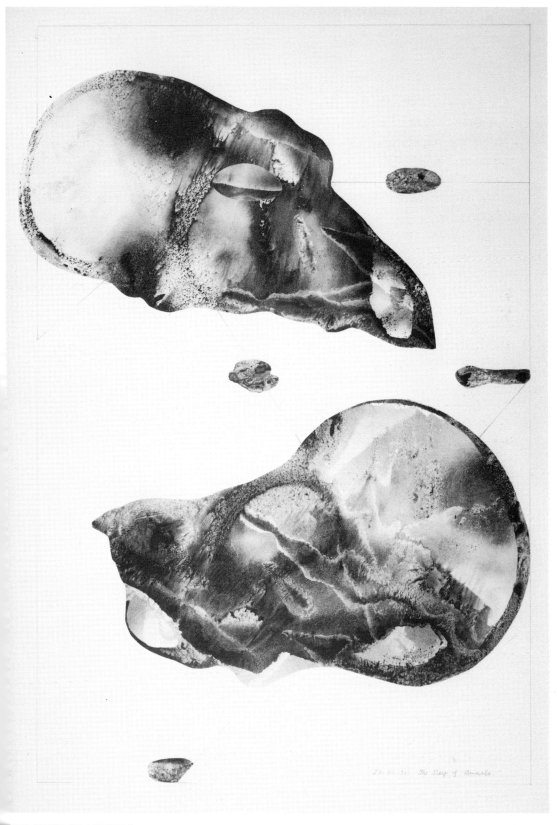

THE SLEEP OF ANIMALS

tears,' says the scientist, 'are a re-creation of the primordial ocean which, in the first stages of evolution, bathed the first eyes.' Perhaps the carnal echo that the contemplation of water awakens in us sounds over those immense distances of time. Or if that thought is too fanciful, when from the ruck and chaos of black paint I find myself paradoxically creating a world of water, light and air, perhaps that same chance is somewhere present in the deed, which led a boy by night along a dark canal in a blackened city and showed him fire unquenchably burning within water.

———

GRAPHICS AND POETRY

AT STOKE

I have lived in a single landscape. Every tone
   And turn have had for their ground
These beginnings in grey-black: a land
   Too handled to be primary – all the same,
The first in feeling. I thought it once
   Too desolate, diminished and too tame
To be the foundation for anything. It straggles
   A haggard valley and lets through
Discouraged greennesses, lights from a pond or two.
   By ash-tips, or where the streets give out
In cindery in-betweens, the hills
   Swell up and free of it to where, behind
The whole vapoury, patched battlefield,
   The cows stand steaming in an acrid wind.
This place, the first to seize on my heart and eye,
   Has been their hornbook and their history.

THE MARL PITS

It was a language of water, light and air
   I sought – to speak myself free of a world
Whose stoic lethargy seemed the one reply
   To horizons and to streets that blocked them back
In a monotone fume, a bloom of grey.
   I found my speech. The years return me
To tell of all that seasoned and imprisoned:
   I breathe familiar, sedimented air
From a landscape of disembowellings, underworlds
   Unearthed among the clay. Digging
The marl, they dug a second nature
   And water, seeping up to fill their pits,
Sheeted them to lakes that wink and shine
   Between tips and steeples, streets and waste
In slow reclaimings, shimmers, balancings,
   As if kindling Eden rescinded its own loss
And words and water came of the same source.

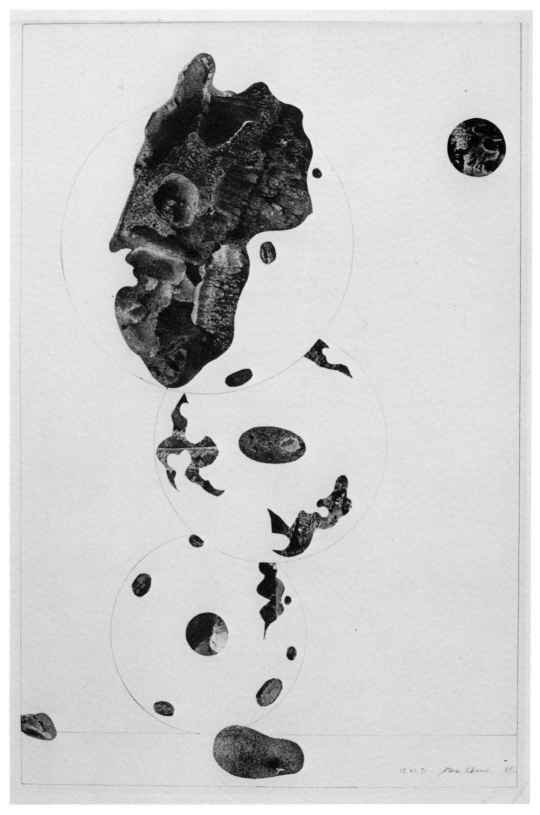

STONE CHRONOS

IN DEFENCE OF METAPHYSICS

Place is the focus. What is the language
Of stones? I do not mean
As emblems of patience, philosophers' hopes
Or as the astrological tangents
One may assemble, draw out subjectively
From a lapidary inertia. Only we
Are inert. Stones act, like pictures, by remaining
Always the same, unmoving, waiting on presence
Unpredictable in absence, inhuman
In a human dependence, a physical
Point of contact, for a movement not physical
And on a track of force, the milestone
Between two infinities. Stones are like deaths.
They uncover limits.

TWO STONES

STONE SPEECH

Crowding this beach
are milkstones, white
teardrops; flints
edged out of flinthood
into smoothness chafe
against grainy ovals,
pitted pieces, nosestones,
stoppers and saddles;
veins of orange
inlay black beads:
chalk-swaddled babyshapes,
tiny fists, facestones
and facestone's brother
skullstone, roundheads
pierced by a single eye,
purple finds, all
rubbing shoulders:
a mob of grindings,
groundlings, scatterings
from a million necklaces
mined under sea-hills, the pebbles
are as various as the people.

TO BE ENGRAVED ON THE SKULL OF A CORMORANT

across the thin
façade, the galleried-
with-membrane head:
narrowing, to take
the eye-dividing
declivity where
the beginning beak
prepares for flight
in a still-
perfect salience:
here, your glass
needs must stay
steady and your gross
needle re-tip
itself with reticence
but be
as searching as the sea
that picked and pared
this head yet spared
its frail acuity.

A GIVEN GRACE

Two cups,
a given grace,
afloat and white
on the mahogany pool
of table. They unclench
the mind, filling it
with themselves.
Though common ware,
these rare reflections,
coolness of brown
so strengthens and refines
the burning of their white,
you would not wish
them other than they are –
you, who are challenged
and replenished by
those empty vessels.

AURICULAR

LOT'S WIFE

SKULLSHAPES

Skulls. Finalities. They emerge towards new beginnings from undergrowth. Along with stones, fossils, flint keel-scrapers and spoke-shaves, along with bowls of clay pipes heel-stamped with their makers' marks, comes the rural detritus of cattle skulls brought home by children. They are moss-stained, filthy with soil. Washing them of their mottlings, the hand grows conscious of weight, weight sharp with jaggednesses. Suspend them from a nail and one feels the bone-clumsiness go out of them: there is weight still in their vertical pull downwards from the nail, but there is also a hanging fragility. The two qualities fuse and the brush translates this fusion as wit, where leg-like appendages conclude the skulls' dangling mass.

Shadow explores them. It sockets the eye-holes with black. It reaches like fingers into the places one cannot see. Skulls are a keen instance of this duality of the visible: it borders what the eye cannot make out, it transcends itself with the suggestion of all that is there beside what lies within the eyes' possession: it cannot be possessed. Flooded with light, the skull is at once manifest surface and labyrinth of recesses. Shadow reaches down out of this world of helmeted cavities and declares it.

One sees. But not merely the passive mirrorings of the retinal mosaic – nor, like Ruskin's blind man struck suddenly by vision, without memory or conception. The senses, reminded by other seeings, bring to bear on the act of vision their pattern of images; they give point and place to an otherwise naked and homeless impression. It is the mind sees. But what it sees consists not solely of that by which it is confronted grasped in the light of that which it remembers. It sees possibility.

The skulls of birds, hard to the touch, are delicate to the eye. Egg-like in the round of the skull itself and as if the spherical shape were the result of an act like glass-blowing, they resist the eyes' imaginings with the blade of the beak which no lyrical admiration can attenuate to frailty.

The skull of nature is recess and volume. The skull of art – of possibility – is recess, volume and also lines – lines of containment, lines of extension. In seeing, one already extends the retinal impression searchingly and instantaneously. Brush and pen extend the search beyond the instant, touch discloses a future. Volume, knived across by the challenge of a line, the raggedness of flaking bone countered by ruled, triangular facets, a cowskull opens a visionary field, a play of universals.

POEM

The muscles which move the eyeballs, we are told, derive from a musculature which once occupied the body end to end . . . Sunblaze as day goes, and the light blots back the scene to iris the half-shut lashes. A look can no longer extricate the centre of the skyline copse. But the last greys, the departing glows caught by the creepers bearding its mass, prevail on the half-blinded retina. Branches deal with the air, vibrating the beams that thread into one's eye. So that 'over there' and 'in here' compound a truce neither signed – a truce that, insensibly and categorically, grows to a decree, and what one hoped for and what one is, must measure themselves against those demands which the eye receives, delivering its writ on us through a musculature which occupies the body end to end.

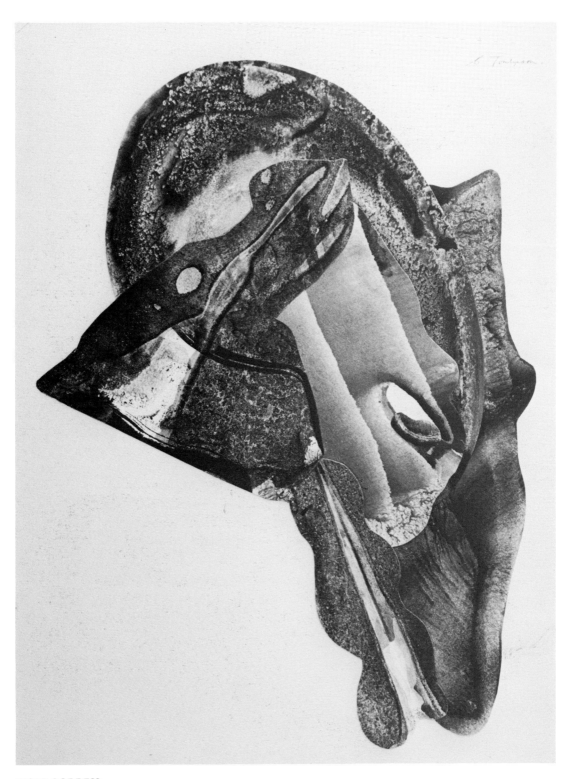

WOLF GODDESS

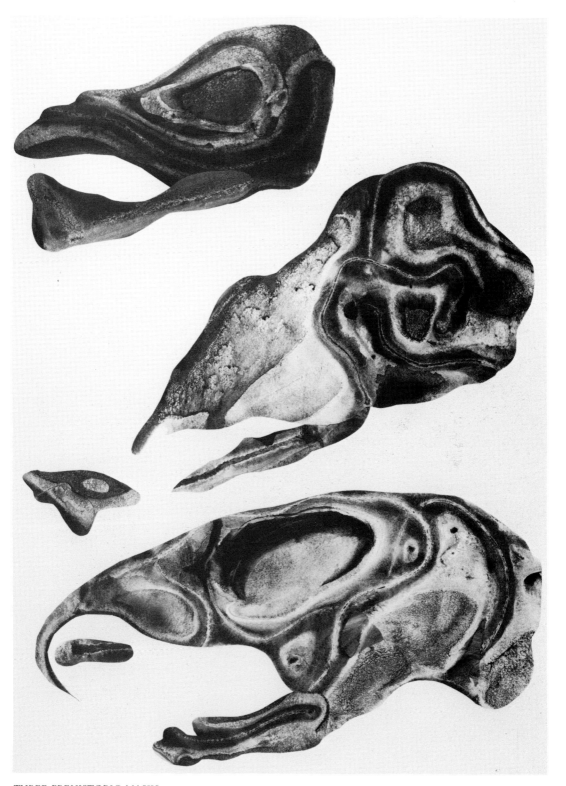

THREE PREHISTORIC MASKS

CÉZANNE AT AIX

And the mountain: each day
Immobile like fruit. Unlike, also
– Because irreducible, because
Neither a component of the delicious
And therefore questionable,
Nor distracted (as the sitter)
By his own pose and, therefore,
Doubly to be questioned: it is not
Posed. It is. Untaught
Unalterable, a stone bridgehead
To that which is tangible
Because unfelt before. There
In its weathered weight
Its silence silences, a presence
Which does not present itself.

PARING THE APPLE

There are portraits and still-lifes.

And there is paring the apple.

And then? Paring it slowly,
From under cool-yellow
Cold-white emerging. And . . .?

The spring of concentric peel
Unwinding off white,
The blade hidden, dividing.

There arc portraits and still-lifes
And the first, because 'human'
Does not excel the second, and
Neither is less weighted
With a human gesture, than paring the apple
With a human stillness.

The cool blade
Severs between coolness, apple-rind
Compelling a recognition.

LIFE IN THE ROCK

CAVE MOUTH

THE CHANCES OF RHYME

The chances of rhyme are like the chances of meeting –
   In the finding fortuitous, but once found, binding:
They say, they signify and they succeed, where to succeed
   Means not success, but a way forward
If unmapped, a literal, not a royal succession;
   Though royal (it may be) is the adjective or region
That we, nature's royalty, are led into.
   Yes. We are led, though we seem to lead
Through a fair forest, an Arden (a rhyme
   For Eden) – breeding ground for beasts
Not bestial, but loyal and legendary, which is more
   Than nature's are. Yet why should we speak
Of art, of life, as if the one were all form
   And the other all Sturm-und-Drang? And I think
Too, we should confine to Crewe or to Mow
   Cop, all those who confuse the fortuitousness
Of art with something to be met with only
   At extremity's brink, reducing thus
Rhyme to a kind of rope's end, a glimpsed grass
   To be snatched as we plunge past it –
Nostalgic, after all, for a hope deferred.
   To take chances, as to make rhymes
Is human, but between chance and impenitence
   (A half-rhyme) come dance, vigilance
And circumstance (meaning all that is there
   Besides you, when you are there). And between
Rest-in-peace and precipice,
   Inertia and perversion, come the varieties
Increase, lease, re-lease (in both
   Senses); and immersion, conversion – of inert
Mass, that is, into energies to combat confusion.
   Let rhyme be my conclusion.

VARIANT ON A SCRAP OF CONVERSATION

'There's nothing at all to be said for the day . . .'

Except that through the wet panes
Objects arrange themselves,
Blue tessellations, faintly irised
Dividing the room
Into an observed music.

As one approaches the windows
Fugues of colour
May be derived from a familiar interior,
A chair may be segmented and reassembled
In two steps.

To challenge the accepted vision
A further instance would be the wine-stopper,
Its head (cut into facets)
An eye for the cubist.

INTO DISTANCE

NEAR YORK

The glistening field has survived its battles:
  A fault in the window-pane takes hold,
Twists to a dip the plain of York:
  But at one shift of the eye the straight
Flows back to occupy that hollow,
  Shadows following ditch and field-line
In horizontals. It is no tyranny
  To the cycle a hedge hides and whose rider
Slotted into the scene, drifts by
  And, making the will of the land his own,
Is wing-swift land-bound. Birds alone
  Can seem to defy the law of the plain:
The lapwings shape out of nothing
  The fells they come dropping through; and their hills
Of air roll with the currents of a wind
  Calling to York from Jorvik as it tries
To speak through this casement where a fault in glass
  Keeps rippling and releasing tense horizons;
As if this place could be pried out of now,
  As if we could fly in the face of all we know.

SKYE LANDSCAPE

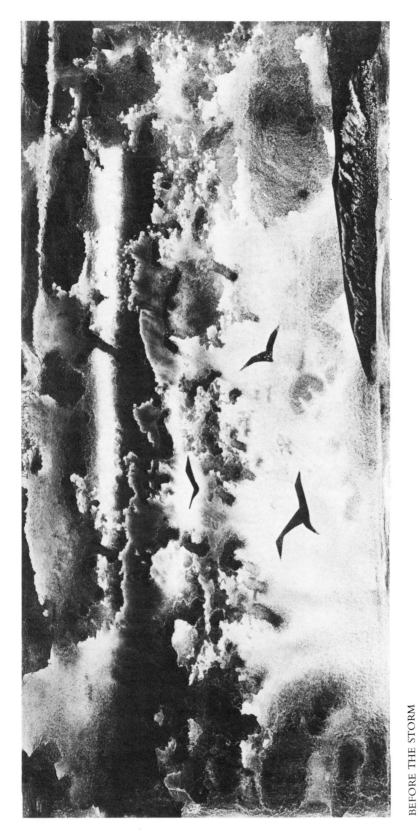

BEFORE THE STORM

THE FARING

That day, the house was so much a ship
   Clasped by the wind, the whole sky
Piling its cloud-wrack past,
   To be sure you were on dry land
You must go out and stand in that stream
   Of air: the entire world out there
Was travelling too: in each gap the tides
   Of space felt for the earth's ship sides:
Over fields, new-turned, the cry
   And scattered constellations of the gulls
Were messengers from that unending sea, the sky:
   White on brown, a double lambency
Pulsed, played where the birds, intent
   On nothing more than the ploughland's nourishment,
Brought the immeasurable in: wing on wing
   Taking new lustres from the turning year
Above seasonable fields, they tacked and climbed
   With a planet's travelling, rhymed here with elsewhere
In the sea-salt freshnesses of tint and air.

PLAGE PAYSAGE

LE RENDEZ-VOUS DES PAYSAGES

The promenade, the plage, the paysage
all met somewhere
in the reflection of a reflection
in midair: cars, unheard,
were running on water: jetplanes
lay on their backs
like sunbathers
in a submarine graveyard
about to resurrect into the fronds
of ghost-palms boasting
'We exist'
to the sea's uncertain mirrors
to the reversed clocktowers that had lost
all feeling for time
suspended
among the overlapping vistas
of promenade, plage, paysage.

MARINE II

MARINE

The water, wind-impelled, advancing
   Along the promontory side, continually
Shaves off into spray, where its flank
   Grazes against rock, each white
In-coming rush like a vast
   Wheel spun to nothing, a wing
Caught down from flight to feathers.

THE FOX GALLERY

A long house –
the fox gallery you called
its upper storey, because
you could look down to see
(and did) the way a fox would
cross the field beyond
and you could follow out, window
to window, the fox's way
the whole length of the meadow
parallel with the restraining line
of wall and pane, or as far
as that could follow the sense of all
those windings. Do you remember
the morning I woke you with the cry
Fox fox and the animal
came on – not from side
to side, but straight
at the house and we craned
to see more and more, the most
we could of it and then
watched it sheer off deterred
by habitation, and saw
how utterly the two worlds were
disparate, as that perfect
ideogram for agility
and liquefaction flowed
away from us rhythmical
and flickering and
that flare was final.

AESTHETIC

Reality is to be sought, not in concrete,
But in space made articulate:
The shore, for instance,
Spreading between wall and wall;
The sea-voice
Tearing the silence from the silence.

Landscape with Bathers   17.V.71.

LANDSCAPE WITH BATHERS

ON WATER

'Furrow' is inexact:
no ship could be
converted to a plough
travelling this vitreous ebony:

seal it in sea-caves and
you cannot still it:
image on image bends
where half-lights fill it

with illegible depths
and lucid passages,
bestiary of stones,
book without pages:

and yet it confers
as much as it denies:
we are orphaned and fathered
by such solid vacancies:

THE FOUR ELEMENTS

ELEMENTAL

A last flame,
sole leaf
flagging at the tree tip,
is dragged through the current
down into the water
of the air, and in this final
metamorphosis, spiralling
swims to earth.

EVENT

Nothing is happening
Nothing

A waterdrop
Soundlessly shatters
A gossamer gives

Against this unused space
A bird
Might thoughtlessly try its voice
But no bird does

On the trodden ground
Footsteps
Are themselves more pulse than sound

At the return
A little drunk
On air

Aware that
Nothing
Is happening

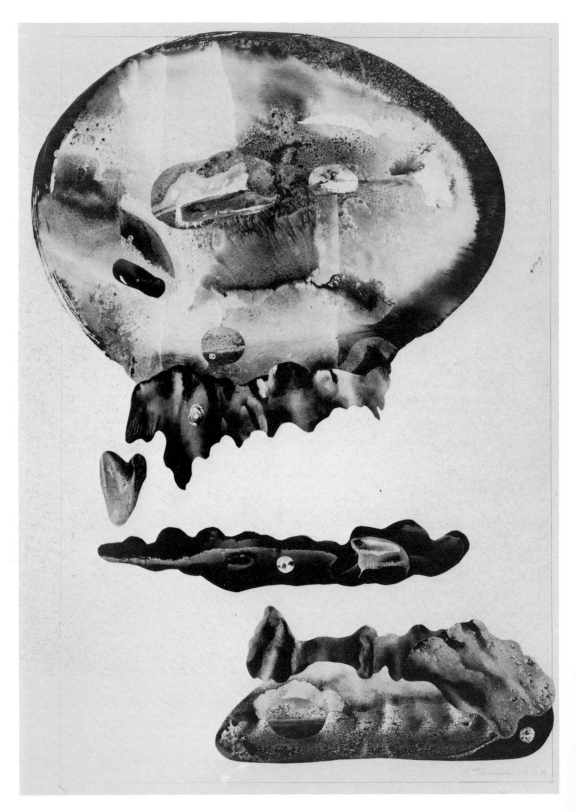

UNTITLED

BETWEEN SEA & SHORE

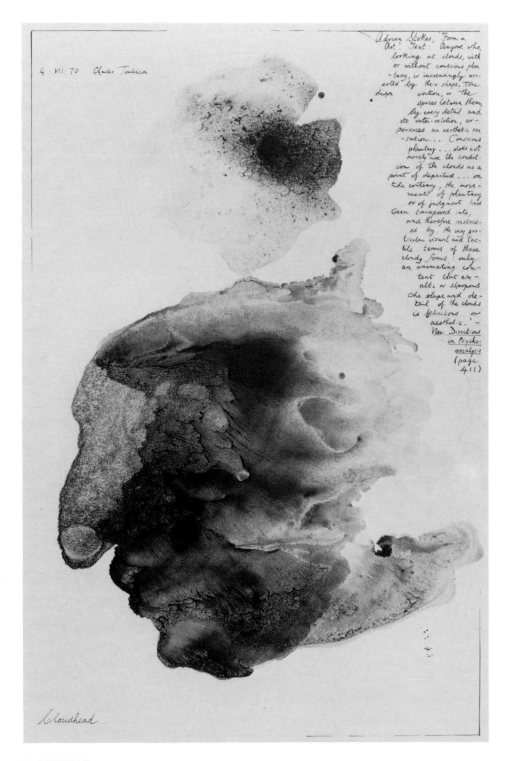

CLOUDHEAD

CLOUDS

How should the dreamer, on those slow
   Solidities, fix his wandering adagio,
Seizing, bone-frail, blown
   Through the diaphanous air of their patrols,
Shadows of fanfares, grails of melting snow?
   How can he hope to hold that white
Opacity as it endures, advances,
   At a dream's length? Its strength
Confounds him with detail, his glance falls
   From ridge to ridge down the soft canyon walls,
And, fleece as it may seem, its tones
   And touch are not the fleece of dream,
But light and body, spaced accumulation
   The mind can take its purchase on:
Cloudshapes are destinies, and they
   Charging the atmosphere of a common day,
Make it the place of confrontation where
   The dreamer wakes to the categorical call
And clear cerulean trumpet of the air.

BIRDS EYE VIEW

IMAGES OF PERFECTION

. . . What do we see
In the perfect thing? Is our seeing
Merely a measuring, a satisfaction
To be compared? How do we know at sight
And for what they are, these rarenesses
That are right? In yesterday's sky
Every variety of cloud accompanied earth,
Mares' tails riding past mountainous anvils,
While their shadows expunged our own:
It was pure display – all a sky could put on
In a single day, and yet remain sky.
I mean, you felt in the air the sway
Of sudden apocalypse, complete revelation:
But what it came to was a lingering
At the edge of time, a perfect neighbouring,
Until the twilight brought it consummation,
Seeping in violet through the entire scene.
Where was the meaning, then? Did Eden
Greet us ungated? Or was that marrying
Purely imaginary and, if it were,
What do we see in the perfect thing?

THE WAY OF A WORLD

Having mislaid it, and then
    Found again in a changed mind
The image of a gull the autumn gust
    Had pulled upwards and past
The window I watched from, I recovered too
    The ash-key, borne-by whirling
On the same surge of air, like an animate thing:
    The scene was there again: the bird,
The seed, the windlines drawn in the sidelong
    Sweep of leaves and branches that only
The black and supple boughs restrained –
    All would have joined in the weightless anarchy
Of air, but for that counterpoise. All rose
    Clear in the memory now, though memory did not choose
Or value it first: it came
    With its worth and, like those tree-tips,
Fine as dishevelling hair, but steadied
    And masted as they are, that worth
Outlasted its lost time, when
    The cross-currents had carried it under.
In all these evanescences of daily air,
    It is the shapes of change, and not the bare
Glancing vibrations, that vein and branch
    Through the moving textures: we grasp
The way of a world in the seed, the gull
    Swayed toiling against the two
Gravities that root and uproot the trees.

EDEN

I have seen Eden. It is a light of place
   As much as the place itself; not a face
Only, but the expression on that face: the gift
   Of forms constellates cliff and stones:
The wind is hurrying the clouds past,
   And the clouds as they flee, ravelling-out
Shadow a salute where the thorn's barb
   Catches the tossed, unroving sack
That echoes their flight. And the same
   Wind stirs in the thicket of the lines
In Eden's wood, the radial avenues
   Of light there, copious enough
To draft a city from. Eden
   Is given one, and the clairvoyant gift
Withdrawn, 'Tell us,' we say
   'The way to Eden,' but lost in the meagre
Streets of our dispossession, where
   Shall we turn, when shall we put down
This insurrection of sorry roofs? Despair
   Of Eden is given, too: we earn
Neither its loss nor having. There is no
   Bridge but the thread of patience, no way
But the will to wish back Eden, this leaning
   To stand against the persuasions of a wind
That rings with its meaninglessness where it sang its meaning.

SEA CAVE

A RETROSPECT

Almost twenty years ago – it was after a third visit to the American Southwest in 1967 – I had a dream.

In this I was walking along a London street and the season was autumn. A smell of leaf-mould tinged the atmosphere, mingling with a touch of frost. The uncertainty and expectation I had experienced before at this season made themselves felt in the dream. Suddenly, at my feet I caught sight of a painting lying on the pavement. As I picked it up, I realised, though I had never seen it before, that it was I who had created it. Two thoughts passed through my mind simultaneously, an instant perception of what seemed to me the completeness of the painting and an almost strained sense of the effort that must have gone into its making.

The same sense of effort returned in the autumn of 1968, after a strenuous and prolonged period of drawing animal and bird skulls. It was only in the summer of 1970 that I re-experienced the sensation of inevitability I had had when contemplating that found picture. This returned in gazing at the images of my first decalcomanias, initiated by me and beyond any conscious intention I might have had – though the excluding of conscious intention was, no doubt, intentional.

That my dream dates from my third visit to New Mexico also has its own significance. I came upon the picture, or it came upon me, with the same unexpectedness and the same sensation of all this occurring after a prolonged search, as I imagine must be felt by the Indian who, in a dream, is given a song by some animal or some numinous power. Living in New Mexico meant that I had not only done some ethnological reading, but that I had attended Indian ceremonies which, if not immediately connected with dreaming, were part and parcel of a cultural tradition in which the dream song held a central place and importance. The hyper-aesthesia and inner concentration which we are told attend upon the giving of the dream song

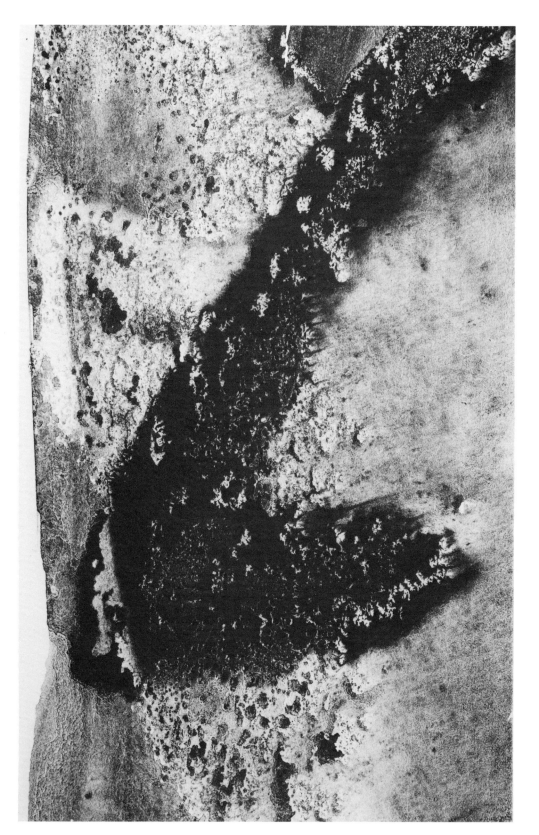

THE SHADOW OF THE HAWK

seemed to be reproduced both in the dream I had had and in what I felt when the forms of my decalcomanias came into view.

I offer this testimony in 'no idle or mystical sense', as the poet says, but as the facts of the situation. I must add to them another. My own tradition as an artist is not, of course, that of the American Indian cults of dance and song, but of European modernism. My chief interest had always been in Cézanne and then in cubism. It was rather to my own surprise that I found myself extending this interest to surrealism. But there had always been one surrealist text which had interested me, ever since I first read it in a book purchased in 1945, and this was Max Ernst's account of his discovery of frottage when, one rainy day at a country inn, he took to transferring the shapes of the wood grain of the floor onto paper by rubbing the spread-out paper with blacklead. Ernst extended this technique by rubbing every conceivable material that happened to come into his field of vision and by combining the results of his frottages to produce finished pictures. In this image-making process, 'the author,' writes Ernst, 'is present as a spectator, indifferent or impassioned, at the birth of his own work.' Neither indifferent nor impassioned – though more impassioned than indifferent – I had been present at the birth of my own work in a dream and, long afterwards, in employment of another technique of Ernst's, decalcomania.

The phase of which I am writing lasted the better part of ten years. The final works produced by means of decalcomania and collage were executed in the early months of 1979. Those ten years, when I was working as poet and painter, possessed a strange radiating sufficiency, both for the large quantity of graphic work I was enabled to produce, and for the effect this had on my writing – namely, of admitting into it a greater regard for chance and for the mysterious fulness of the given. Though I have ceased to make pictures I feel that my poems still lie open to forces emanating from that now completed phase. It seems, in retrospect, to have been like a season in Eden.

CT
1985

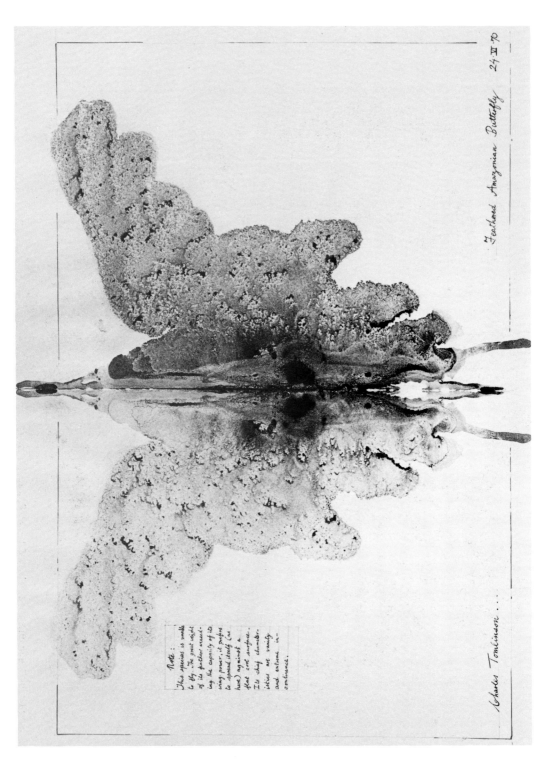

Note:
This species is unable to fly. The great weight of its feather circulating the capacity of its wing power, it prefers to spread itself (in turn) against a flat cool surface. Its chief characteristics are vanity and extreme in-exuberance.

Feathered Amazonian Butterfly 24·IV·70

Charles Tomlinson...

FEATHERED AMAZONIAN BUTTERFLY

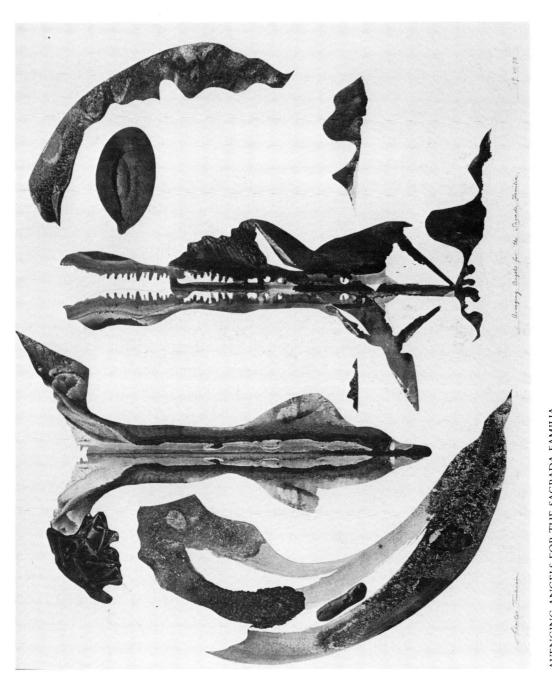

Charles Timbrell

Avenging Angels for the Sagrada Familia.

18.vii.73

AVENGING ANGELS FOR THE SAGRADA FAMILIA

LIST OF POEMS

LIST OF GRAPHICS

Measurements in millimetres

BIBLIOGRAPHY

Relations and Contraries (Aldington, Kent: Hand & Flower Press, 1951);

The Necklace (Oxford: Fantasy Press, 1955; revised edition, London & New York: Oxford University Press, 1966);

Seeing is Believing (New York: McDowell, Obolensky, 1958; London: Oxford University Press, 1960);

Versions from Fyodor Tyutchev, 1803–1873, with an introduction by Henry Gifford (London: Oxford University Press, 1960);

A Peopled Landscape (London & New York: Oxford University Press, 1963);

Castilian Ilexes: Versions from Machado, by Tomlinson and Henry Gifford (London & New York: Oxford University Press, 1963);

Poems: A Selection, by Tomlinson, Tony Connor and Austin Clarke (London & New York: Oxford University Press, 1964);

American Scenes and Other Poems (London & New York: Oxford University Press, 1966);

The Poem as Initiation (Hamilton N.Y.: Colgate University Press, 1968);

The Matachines: New Mexico (Cerillos, N.M.: San Marcos Press, 1968);

To Be Engraved on the Skull of a Cormorant (London: The Unaccompanied Serpent, 1968);

Penguin Modern Poets 14, by Tomlinson, Alan Brownjohn, and Michael Hamburger (Harmondsworth: Penguin, 1969);

The Way of a World (London & New York: Oxford University Press, 1969);

America West Southwest (Cerillos, N.M.: San Marcos Press, 1969);

Ten Versions from Trilce, by Tomlinson and Gifford (Cerillos, N.M.: San Marcos Press, 1974);

Words and Images (London: Covent Garden Press, 1972);

Written on Water (London: Oxford University Press, 1972);

Renga: a Chain of Poems by Octavio Paz, Jacques Roubaud, Edoardo Sanguineti, and Tomlinson, English translations by Tomlinson (New York: Braziller, 1972; Penguin, 1979);

The Way in and Other Poems (London, New York & Toronto: Oxford University Press, 1974);

In Black and White (Cheadle, Cheshire: Carcanet Press, 1976);

Selected Poems 1951–74 (Oxford & New York: Oxford University Press, 1978);

The Shaft (Oxford & New York: Oxford University Press, 1978);

Airborn/Hijos del Aire (with Octavio Paz) London: Anvil Press, 1981);

The Flood (Oxford & New York: Oxford University Press, 1981);

Some Americans: a Personal Record (Berkeley, Los Angeles & London: University of California Press, 1981);

Isaac Rosenberg of Bristol (Bristol: The Historical Association, 1982);

Poetry and Metamorphosis (Cambridge: Cambridge University Press, 1983);

The Sense of the Past: Three Twentieth Century British Poets (Liverpool: Liverpool University Press, 1983);

Translations (Oxford: Oxford University Press, 1983);

Notes from New York and Other Poems (Oxford: Oxford University Press, 1984).

Collected Poems (Oxford: Oxford University Press, 1985).

Note: This list does not include anthologies edited by Charles Tomlinson.

OTHER BOOKS FROM REDCLIFFE

Dutch Alps

James Hamilton-Paterson

The author's second full length collection presents work rich in alien and exotic settings. At times surrealistically challenging, at others poignantly lyrical, his finely wrought work repeatedly undermines and unsettles the security of literal perception.

"Considerable technical ability and a lively intellectual complexity . . . a decidedly original collection" *British Book News*

"This is undoubtedly poetry of considerable intelligence and, at its best, of a startling sensory perception" *Anglo-Welsh Review*

ISBN 0 905459 80 6   64pp   £3.00

From the Red Fort

Francis Berry

This is the first comprehensive selection of Francis Berry's work. Also assembled here are three previously unpublished long poems (one commissioned by the BBC) and a number of new short pieces.

"It is questionable whether any contemporary poet can offer so great a range of technique and subject matter" *Philip Hobsbaum*, Tradition and Experiment in English Poetry.

ISBN 0 905459 96 2   94pp   £3.95

Vision and Death of Aubrey Beardsley

Derek Stanford

In this unique dramatic monologue, Derek Stanford brings the world's most notorious black and white artist back to life.

Closely based on biographical fact, even at times employing the artist's own words, the author traces his obsessions with art, sex and later, Catholicism. We witness his brushes with Oscar Wilde, John Lane and the turbulent passage of the Yellow Book.

This psychological reconstruction, nourished by the author's special knowledge of the period, produces a portrait, a poem, which reaches beyond traditional limits.

ISBN 0 905459 85 7   80pp   Fully illustrated   £4.95

Henry Lamb: The Artist and his Friends

Keith Clements

The full story of Lamb's life and an assessment of his work is long overdue.

The man and the artist have been rediscovered from a wealth of unpublished material and extensive interviews with family, friends and collectors. It is a remarkably frank and intimate portrait of a very private person and is a critical biography which fills a significant and considerable gap in the life and letters of the period.

The story sheds new light on Bloomsbury and Fitzrovia, and Lamb's turbulent relationship with Lytton Strachey, Ottoline Morrell, Virginia Woolf and Stanley Spencer are spotlighted for the first time.

"An engrossing portrait of a complex man" Frances Spalding, *Country Life*

"A fascinating study . . . a model of how such an enquiry should be conducted." Paul Johnson, *The Spectator*

ISBN 0 905459 55   352pp   Fully illustrated Casebound   £16.50

Writers in Sussex

Bernard Smith and Peter Haas

Foreword by Christopher Fry

No English county has a richer or more varied literary heritage than Sussex. This textual/photographic collaboration is both a celebration and guide to over forty writers who have lived in the county.

The cast list is surprising. Topping the bill are writers like Tennyson, Keats, Conan Doyle, Yeats, Blake, Virginia Woolf, Kipling, John Cowper Powys, A.A. Milne. But there are intriguing discoveries of names little known today but who were celebrated in their own times.

As Christopher Fry says: "what better guide in Sussex than Bernard Smith? The wide county from east to west has been given a fresh reason for us to explore, to visit those places so splendidly caught by the camera of Peter Haas"

ISBN 0 905459 97 0   120pp   Fully illustrated   £4.95